The Calling to
Manhood

Richard Harris

© Copyright 2024 – Richard Harris

Printed in the United States of America. All rights reserved. No portion of this book may be reproduced, stored in a retrieval system, or transmitted in any form or by any means—electronic, mechanical, photocopy, recording, scanning, or other—except for brief quotations in critical reviews or articles, without the prior written permission of the publisher.

Unless otherwise indicated, all Scripture quotations are taken from the King James Version® of the Bible. Copyright © by the British Crown. Public domain.

Scripture taken from the New King James Version®. Copyright © 1982 by Thomas Nelson. Used by permission. All rights reserved.

All emphasis within Scripture quotations is the author's own.

Published by Truth and Liberty Foundation, Inc., an integrated auxiliary of Andrew Wommack Ministries, Inc.

Woodland Park, CO 80863

ISBN 13 TP: 978-1-7372113-2-7

For Worldwide Distribution, Printed in the USA

1 2 3 4 5 6 / 27 26 25 24

Contents

Introduction 1

Chapter 1 What Is Manhood? 5

Chapter 2 The Call to Lead! 15

Chapter 3 The Call to Fight! 23

Chapter 4 The Call to Work! 37

Conclusion 47

Introduction

Nearly 250 years ago at a meeting hall in Philadelphia, Pennsylvania, fifty-six men entered the valley of decision.[1] As delegates from the thirteen American Colonies, they gathered to consider what course of action they should take after "a long train of abuses" from a tyrannical government had increasingly encroached on their freedoms and threatened to remove them once and for all. The British army and navy had laid siege to Boston and the Americans were resisting. Peace with Britain was still possible, but at what price? As leaders and ministers in their communities, these men had been preaching, based on the Bible, that God made all men free and equal. Now the time had come for them to decide whether to declare independence and start their own nation: Did they really believe in the things they preached? They knew their decision could mean the loss of everything they held dear—their families, their homes, and even their own lives. But they also knew that the extreme crisis presented them, and all Americans, a chance of a better life.

In previous years, these men had engaged in civil disobedience, standing to be counted again and again for freedom in America. But they took their most daring leap by far when they signed the Declaration of Independence, possibly the greatest piece of political writing ever penned. They knew that when they put their names on that piece of paper they were committing treason in the eyes of the King, and if they were to lose the war, they would all be executed. When the Continental Congress met to vote on declaring independence from Great Britain, one founder advised the delegates that to prevail they must all "hang together." Benjamin Franklin, a delegate from Pennsylvania, quipped, "We must, indeed, all hang together, or most assuredly we shall all hang separately."[2]

What makes their actions in signing the Declaration so incredible is that they had no reason to hope for success—in the natural. The British army was the largest and most powerful in the world as was the British navy. In contrast, America had virtually no navy and only a fledgling army under the command of fellow patriot, George Washington. The brand-new confederation of colonies had no allies, little money in its treasury, and few supplies. But these fifty-six men, whom we now call America's "Founding Fathers," placed their faith in God and did what their consciences and their convictions told them had to be done, even if it meant great cost to themselves. I submit to you that these men were obeying God's calling to true manhood.

One of the Founding Fathers, Thomas Nelson Jr., owned a home in Virginia. According to oral tradition, during the famous final battle of the Revolutionary War at Yorktown, he came upon an artillery battery of the Continental Army and noticed that they were not firing toward the house where General Cornwallis of the British had set up his headquarters. Nelson said to the artillery officer, "Why aren't you firing on Cornwallis?" They told him, "Sir, because it's your house!" He walked right up to the cannon, turned it toward his house, and told them, "Begin firing." They destroyed his home! I want to suggest to you that he, and other men like him, were able to do things like this because they were walking in the calling of God to true manhood.

These courageous men didn't just sign a piece of paper and hope for the best; they followed through on their convictions. At this time in history, only twenty percent of the American public was in favor of the Declaration.[3] Being moved by what was right, not by public opinion, these fifty-six men worked tirelessly for years until their vision became a reality. The courageous decision they made on that fateful

July day at Independence Hall nearly 250 years ago, and their determined commitment to see it through, birthed what would become the greatest nation the world has ever known.

Today in America, we are faced again with challenges that are not dissimilar to the ones that the signers of the Declaration of Independence faced. As it was in 1776, today we need men of courage, integrity, and dedication to step up and not step aside! We need a remnant of men from this generation, for the sake of our families, our communities, and our beloved country, who will rise to the biblical calling of what it really means to be men. Unless we answer the call to manhood, there is no guarantee that America will continue to survive.

With this booklet, I am issuing a call to men everywhere who love America. The Lord gave me three charges to share that I believe are critical for this time in history. Our freedom and Christian heritage are at stake, and we as men must answer the call. If we don't, no one else will. The responsibility is ours!

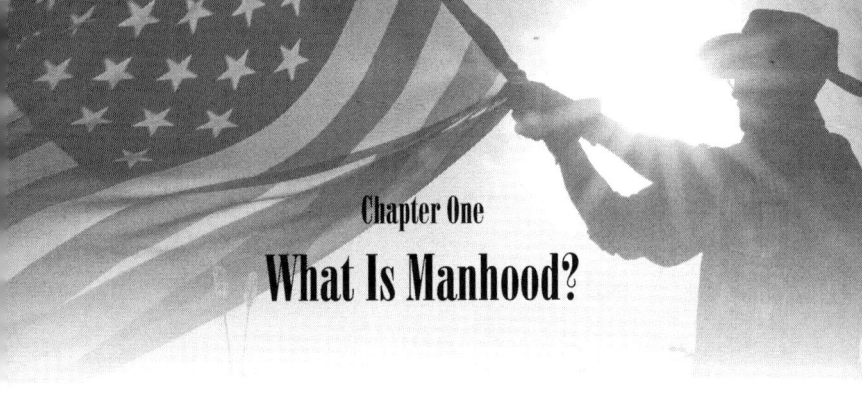

Chapter One
What Is Manhood?

America became the greatest nation the world has ever known because our Founding Fathers walked in the call of God to true manhood.

But what is true manhood? Are all males that reach a certain age automatically men? Is it based on appearance: stature, muscle mass, or facial hair? No, none of these things are what I am referring to when I refer to true manhood. What I am suggesting to you is that true manhood exists on the inside of a man. I am talking about the heart. True manhood is about a man's mindset, his convictions, and his character.

In ancient Israel, God raised up a prophet named Samuel, who ministered during the reign of Israel's first king, Saul. Saul disobeyed the Lord because he loved the approval of the people more than the approval of God (1 Samuel 13). God rejected Saul from being king and led Samuel to anoint a new king of Israel. The Lord told Samuel he was seeking "*a man after mine own heart*" (1 Sam. 13:14 and Acts 13:22). He sent Samuel to the family of Jesse in Bethlehem. Jesse had eight sons and brought the oldest seven of them before the prophet. Samuel first tried to anoint Eliab, the oldest of Jesse's eight sons. But God said no, telling Samuel,

> *Look not on his countenance, or on the height of his stature; because I have refused him: for the LORD seeth not as man seeth; for man looketh on the outward appearance, but* **the LORD looketh on the heart**.
>
> 1 Samuel 16:7

Then, one by one, the Lord had Samuel pass over each of Jesse's seven sons until there were none left. Then, when asked, Jesse said there was one more, the youngest, who was tending to the sheep (1 Sam. 16:11-12). Samuel told him to have him come. It was then that he met and anointed David to be king of Israel, "*in the midst of his brethren*"(1 Sam. 16:13).

Manhood in the eyes of God is about the heart. It has nothing to do with outward appearances.

Consider what the Bible says in 1 Corinthians 16:13:

Watch ye, stand fast in the faith, quit you like men, be strong.

The word "*quit*" in Old English does not mean to stop doing something; it actually means "to be brave".[4] So, Paul is telling us to act bravely like men!

Let that sink in for a second. "Isn't it politically incorrect to say this today?" someone will ask. Yes, it certainly is, and that's part of the problem.

Our culture has been demeaning men and manhood for decades now. We are at a point where many people don't even know what it means to be a man and think that masculinity is "toxic." But God Almighty in the Holy Scriptures said for men to stand up and act like men. We need to ignore "political correctness" and agree with God!

God Made Male and Female

Because of the incredibly confused culture we're living in today, we must rebuild the foundation God originally established. In Genesis 1:27–28, we read,

> *So God created man in his own image, in the image of God created he him; male and female created he them. And God blessed them, and God said unto them, Be fruitful, and multiply, and replenish the earth, and subdue it: and have dominion over the fish*

of the sea, and over the fowl of the air, and over every living thing that moveth upon the earth.

Then we see in Genesis 2,

And the Lord God said, It is not good that the man should be alone; I will make him an help meet for him . . . And the Lord God caused a deep sleep to fall upon Adam, and he slept: and he took one of his ribs, and closed up the flesh instead thereof; And the rib, which the Lord God had taken from man, made he a woman, and brought her unto the man.

Genesis 2:18 and 21–22

I'm sure you have heard these verses before. They're taught every week in Sunday school at churches around the world. But today's culture either doesn't know or doesn't believe these passages. As Christ's disciples, devoted to the authority of His Word, we need to stand strong in the truth that God made man and woman from the beginning, and the two are not the same! They have distinct differences that go beyond just the physical.

Today people say, "Oh, you can just go have surgery and change your gender. You can take some drugs manufactured in a laboratory and—*poof*—you're a man or a woman." They want you to believe it's just that easy. But that's utter nonsense. Sex is genetic. It's chromosomal. There is a specific pair of chromosomes that determines sex and they exist from the moment of conception. These chromosomes do not change but remain the same for life. For men, there is an X and a Y chromosome. For women, there are two X chromosomes. This is a basic reality of biology in every single cell of virtually every human being. Plainly stated, every person's sex is programmed by God.

Researchers have documented over 6,000 variations in human biology between males and females that result from this genetic difference.[5]

Transgender ideologues today claim that sex is merely "assigned" by humans when a baby is born, but that it is really "fluid" and "nonbinary." This is absolutely and obviously untrue. Sex is not "assigned" by anyone at birth. Sex is a fixed, biological fact that is plain and obvious. Doctors can give drugs and surgery to alter *outward appearances*, but they can't change a person's sex. Fake hormones, hormone blockers, and mutilating surgery only mask the truth. They create an appearance of a different sex, but they do not change a person's actual sex. Further, the fact that a man may choose to dress like a woman, wear makeup, and use female pronouns does not mean he is a woman. It only means he is *pretending* to be a woman. God made us male and female, and no human being can change that. No one can make a man into a woman or a woman into a man. Maleness and femaleness are part of our fundamental design.

The Devil's Attack on Identity

Satan is robbing the men of our nation of their calling to manhood. People are so confused today that they can no longer define a person's sex. They think it's not real, that it's not fixed at birth. They think it's something you can choose. They think that whatever you feel, or "identify" with on a given day, determines your gender.

How did we get here? It all started when people began to mock and ridicule the traditional roles of men and women, claiming there was no difference between the sexes. So-called "feminists" claimed, "women can do anything men can do."

For decades now, our culture has been shaming women for being feminine and shaming men for being masculine. Men are told, "You need to be more sensitive. You need to talk more. You need to be in touch with your feelings." I remember Hillary Clinton sitting on the set of *60 Minutes* in the 1990s.[6] She was making fun of women who chose to stay home and raise their children. It's progressed now to the point that it's not enough for people to have the freedom in this great nation to call *themselves* whatever sex they want; now they're trying to force all of us to *agree* with them!

Intimidation is a major tool of the enemy. Many once-trusted institutions in our country, like the Department of Justice and the FBI, have been weaponized against Bible-believing Christians. So, on top of all the madness, Christians have to deal with the fear of speaking up and standing for truth, lest they risk the system coming down on them to cancel, ridicule, or marginalize them. As a result, they've gotten comfortable with remaining silent at a time when their voices are needed the most. Even men, who are called to be protectors, have not been immune to this new form of tyranny. Instead of standing up with conviction for the sake of their families and their communities, they have slidden into indifference, inaction, and cowardice.

Today, sane people are called oppressors, while twisted and confused people are called heroes. When Bruce Jenner underwent surgery and came out as Caitlyn Jenner, he was praised for his courage. Jill Biden recently gave the International **Woman** of Courage Award to a male who pretends to be a woman.[7] The NCAA is allowing men to compete in women's sports just because they want to pretend to be women, with no regard for how unfair that is for true women.[8] Recently, a mentally and emotionally broken young woman who claimed to be a man went into a Christian school in Nashville, Tennessee, and killed six innocent people including children.[9] After that, the White House appallingly said that it's the *trans* people in this nation who are under attack, declaring a national "Transgender Day of Visibility."[10]

The devil has used our confusion on these matters as a Trojan horse to destroy us left, right, and center. Jesus said that "*the thief cometh not, but for to steal, and to kill, and to destroy*" (John 10:10). I'm here to tell you that we are under a satanic attack! But the devil can only devour those who will let him devour them (1 Pet. 5:8).

We need to realize that what we're dealing with is the same thing Jesus dealt with during His life and ministry. The Pharisees perverted the Word of God to advance their own selfish agenda. Jesus told them, "*Ye are of your father the devil, and the lusts of your father ye will do. He was a murderer from the beginning, and abode not in the truth, because there is no truth in him. When he speaketh a lie, he speaketh of his own: for he is a liar, and the father of it*" (John 8:44).

What He spoke to the Pharisees is just as applicable to the "woke" LGBT ideology that is being forced on us today. It is a lying deception that is rooted in the lust, greed, and envy that flows from the hearts of deceived and wounded people.

This whole construct to strip people of their God-given identities is a huge lie designed by Satan. It's what he's always done. When he tempted Adam and Eve, he told them that by eating the fruit of the Tree of Knowledge of Good and Evil, they would become like God (Gen. 3:4–5). He was trying to confuse them. But here's the thing: They were already like God! In fact, they were more like Him before they ate the fruit than after they ate it. It was all an attack on their God-given identities.

The same could be said of when Satan tempted Jesus. After God announced to everyone that Jesus was the beloved Son of God (Matt. 3:17), the devil came to tempt Him. Satan began two of his temptations with "*if thou be the Son of God*" (Matt. 4:3 and 4:6). Once again, he tries to make us doubt our identity. The devil doesn't have any new tricks; he uses the same old junk he's thrown at man since the beginning. He wants to rob us of our destiny, purpose, and calling. He's always using intimidation, confusion, and fear to try to infiltrate and destroy us. We must beware "*lest Satan should get an advantage of us: for we are not ignorant of his devices*" (2 Cor. 2:11).

Divine Purpose in Gender Roles

The truth is when God created us male and female, He said it was very good (Gen. 1:31). He said it was very good because He had a glorious purpose in what He created. We need to accept and appreciate all the wonderful things He has done.

As it relates to manhood, I believe there are three acts that real men are called to do. I hope and pray that something would arise within the heart of every man reading this booklet that would cause him to stand up in this generation to fulfill that calling.

But I'm also talking to the women who might be reading too. Women need to understand what's going on inside the heart of the men God is raising up. It's important for them to understand that they actually have a critical role to play in men taking their proper place. In the following chapters, I will be sharing how men are made, how they're programmed, and what they're designed to do. I believe this will help women to stop trying to pull them down from that calling, but instead, to support and elevate them to embrace it.

Chapter Two
The Call to Lead!

The first thing that God designed a man to do is to lead. This is a biblical concept that we as a society need to understand. One of the reasons the world is in the state it's in, with all this confusion, is because we've refused to accept the way God made us. But the Bible says that *"Adam was formed first, then Eve"* (1 Tim. 2:13, *NKJV*).

When Eve was tempted to eat the forbidden fruit, it says she took it, ate, and "gave it to her husband who was with her and he did eat" (Gen. 3:6). At that moment, Adam failed to walk in his calling to lead. The Scriptures teach that it was through Adam's action that sin entered the world, and through sin, death (Rom. 5:12-14). In a sense, the failure of the first man to lead is the root cause of all problems in the world today!

Now, at its core, leadership is really just influence, and God has designed every single man to influence others. Jesus told His disciples in Matthew 28:19–20 (*NKJV*),

> *Go therefore and make disciples of all the nations, baptizing them in the name of the Father and of the Son and of the Holy Spirit, teaching them to observe all things that I have commanded you; and lo, I am with you always,* even *to the end of the age.*

These were some of Jesus' final words before His ascension. It is known as "the Great Commission," and it's a commandment to influence others for Christ.

Salt and Light

True manhood and real leadership mean doing what is right and speaking up for the truth even when it costs you. Anyone who calls himself a man but isn't willing to speak the truth because he fears the personal consequences is not walking in manhood. Jesus said in Matthew 5:13, "*Ye are the salt of the earth: but if the salt have lost his savour, wherewith shall it be salted? It is thenceforth good for nothing, but to be cast out, and to be trodden under foot of men.*" When salt is poured into a wound, it stings, doesn't it? So, when you're standing up and being salt in this culture, you shouldn't be surprised that people don't want to hear what you have to say.

Jesus went on to say, "*Ye are the light of the world. A city that is set on an hill cannot be hid. Neither do men light a candle, and put it under a bushel, but on a candlestick; and it giveth light unto all that are in the house. Let your light so shine before men, that they may see your good works, and glorify your Father which is in heaven*" (Matt. 5:14–16). If you go into a dark room where someone is sleeping and you flip on the light, how are they going to react? "Argh! Turn that off," right? People who are in darkness often don't want the light turned on.

Jesus Himself faced the same problem. John 3:16-17 tells us that God gave His Son Jesus because He loves the world, not to condemn the world.

> *For God so loved the world, that he gave his only begotten Son, that whosoever believeth in him should not perish, but have everlasting life. For God sent not his Son into the world to condemn the world; but that the world through him might be saved.*

But just two verses later, the Bible says that many people rejected Jesus because He is Light and His light exposed their evil deeds.

> *And this is the condemnation, that light is come into the world, and men loved darkness rather than light, because their deeds were evil. For every one that doeth evil hateth the light, neither cometh to the light, lest his deeds should be reproved.*
>
> John 3:19-20

The fact that Jesus faced rejection never stopped Him from speaking the truth and doing what was right. And, if we are going to walk in our calling to true manhood, the same must be true for each of us. We have Christ's light inside of us, and God is calling every man who believes in Him to shine that light.

To be salt and light in this generation, you will need to be a man of integrity, willing to stand up for truth whether it is popular or profitable. Jesus spoke to the leaders of His day and called them hypocrites and whitewashed tombs (Matt. 23:27). True biblical leaders are men who hate covetousness and love truth (Ex. 18:21). There is a big problem in America today with covetousness, and it's no wonder that it's so rare to find men of integrity. When you look at the corruption that is in this nation, the reason there's so much lying, deception, and wickedness is because men are in love with money (1 Tim. 6:10)! Think about that.

The fifty-six men who signed the Declaration of Independence took a stand, regardless of cost or compensation, and the world has never been the same since. You and I are living in the light of what they did. There is a desperate need for leadership like that again in today's world.

You may think, "well, they were different. They were significant, intelligent, wealthy men. I'm not like that." If that's how you think, you are believing a lie. Every single person, no matter how great or how small, has an area of influence. Who are the people around you? Are you intentionally influencing them toward God? Don't say, "I'm not a leader." Leaders aren't born; they are made. Leading others is a choice. Leaders are men who choose to be like Christ, follow Him, and obey Him. Christ left the glory, wealth, and praise of heaven to come into a dark world so He could stand up for truth. Jesus said in John 18:37, "*For this cause came I into the world, that I should bear witness unto the truth.*" Can you lay aside your desire for acclaim and this world's comforts and stand for the truth? Then you can walk in true manhood just like Christ.

Great Leaders Are Great Fathers

George Washington is one of the greatest leaders ever. But he wasn't born a leader. The truth is that he committed himself to Christ and then disciplined himself mentally and physically to live a virtuous life. He started as an apprentice in surveying. He became a vestryman at his church. He also served in the British army and spent fifteen years in the Virginia legislature. All this happened before he became a General in the American Revolutionary War or became the first President of the United States.[11] He earned the title of "father" of this country because of his commitment to godly character; namely, humility, honor, gentleness, manners, courage, and truthfulness. These are the qualities that gained him the respect of his peers.

The calling to manhood begins first at home. The Bible says,

> *Fathers, provoke not your children to wrath: but bring them up in the nurture and admonition of the Lord.*
> Ephesians 6:4

There is a fatherhood crisis in America today. Over 18 million kids in America today live in fatherless homes.[12] That's one out of every four children. But, if we want to solve that problem, we have to realize that, fundamentally, it's really not a fatherhood crisis; it's a manhood crisis. The lack of fathers in the home is because people don't understand, and don't want to accept, what real manhood is. Let me share a few statistics with you:

- According to a study done by the America First Policy Institute, children who live in fatherless homes are nine times more likely to drop out of school, twice as likely to suffer from mental health issues, and five times more likely to have mood disorders.

- Sixty-three percent of youth suicides are committed by kids whose dads are not living in the home.

- Children without fathers in the home are twenty times more likely to end up in jail and 279 percent more likely to carry guns and deal drugs.

- Eighty-two percent of school shootings are committed by young people who do not have a father in the home.

The Left is telling us today, "Oh, the problems in society are because of racism. It's because of economic disparities. We need affirmative action. We need welfare. We need free college. We need gun control." They are totally wrong. We don't need any of that. What we need is a revival of manhood in the hearts and minds of the men of our nation, including a restoration of the values of sexual morality, sacrifice, and duty.

Manhood is first a calling to lead our families. But it is also more than that. Too many men in this country think, *If I just go to work, do a good job, and then come home, I've done my duty. I'm providing for my family, aren't I?* Well, that's good, and if every man in America did that, we would definitely be better off! But our duty as men does not start and stop at our front doors. It's bigger than that! To respond to the calling of true manhood, you must answer some more questions: What are you doing today to influence your community? What about your church? What about your neighbors? What about your workplace? Are you quiet when people around you are embracing and supporting lies? Have you examined your life and asked yourself, "How can I influence others in my circle?" As a man, God is calling you to lead any and everywhere you can. There are no exceptions. Man, embrace your place as an influencer, and do not underestimate the impact you can make. You can make a real and eternal difference!

Chapter Three
The Call to Fight!

The second call God has given men is to fight. I understand that a good man is generally called a "gentleman." But a true gentleman is not only one who is patient and kind and honors women around him. He is also someone who will fight to defend women and all those around him who are weak and vulnerable. A real gentleman is no coward. He knows when it's time to put on the uniform and pick up his gun to defend what is true and dear.

It is inherent in men to have a combative side to them when those they love are threatened. Why is that? Men are designed to fight. God gave men the heart and ability to fight, not for destructive purposes, but for constructive purposes. A mature man will understand the difference between "*a time to kill, and a time to heal; a time to break down, and a time to build up*" (Eccl. 3:3). God has not only given men a call to fight, but He has *designed* them to fight. It's a part of their manhood, and the world today needs it!

Now, when we talk about fighting for constructive purposes, we're talking about protecting the weak and the vulnerable and defending our families and our nation. Most of the great figures in the Old Testament were either warriors or they led armies in battle. Abraham went and destroyed five kings to save his nephew Lot (Gen. 14:1–16). Then you have Moses who led the Israelites against the Amalekites (Ex. 17:8–13). And how about Joshua who led Israel into the Promised Land to face giants? That's not to mention all the judges who fought in battle after battle to deliver Israel from her enemies.

I was really blessed recently when I attended an event at Charis Bible College in Woodland Park, Colorado, to designate the campus as part of "The Purple Heart Trail." The Purple Heart is a military award that recognizes the merit and valor of members of our armed services who are wounded by the enemy in combat. The Purple Heart Trail is a program where organizations can erect a sign that honors all the recipients of this award in our nation's history. At this ceremony, three veterans spoke. They all served with special forces in the Vietnam War and were wounded in combat. One of them read what he called the official prayer of the Green Beret, now known as the Special Forces Prayer. The prayer reads as follows:

> Almighty God, Who art the Author of liberty and the Champion of the oppressed, hear our prayer.

We the men of Special Forces, acknowledge our dependence upon Thee in the preservation of human freedom. Go with us as we seek to defend the defenseless and to free the enslaved.

May we ever remember that our nation, whose oath "In God We Trust" expects that we shall acquit ourselves with honor, that we may never bring shame upon our faith, our families, or our fellow men.

Grant us wisdom from Thy mind, courage from Thine heart, and protection by Thine hand. It is for Thee that we do battle, and to Thee belongs the victor's crown, for Thine is the kingdom, and the power and Glory forever. AMEN[13]

This prayer really impacted me. It perfectly captures the calling of God to fight. The God-given desire to fight is not for revenge or personal gain, but "to defend the defenseless and to free the enslaved," and to bring honor to God and those they love.

It's important to realize that while the calling of God to man to fight includes the right to conduct just physical warfare, it is really much broader than that. 2 Corinthians 10:3-5 tells us that all followers of Christ are engaged in an unseen war that rages in the spirit realm:

For though we walk in the flesh, we do not war after the flesh: (For the weapons of our warfare are not carnal, but mighty through God to the pulling down of strong holds;) Casting down imaginations, and every high thing that exalteth itself against the knowledge of God, and bringing into captivity every thought to the obedience of Christ;

Ephesians 6:10-17 tells us that our real enemy in this fight is Satan and his dark forces. We are instructed to fight this fight in the spirit with God's weapons and the Lord's strength:

Finally, my brethren, be strong in the Lord, and in the power of his might. Put on the whole armour of God, that ye may be able to stand against the wiles of the devil. For we wrestle not against flesh and blood, but against principalities, against powers, against the rulers of the darkness of this world, against spiritual wickedness in high places. Wherefore take unto you the whole armour of God, that ye may be able to withstand in the evil day, and having done all, to stand. Stand therefore, having your loins girt about with truth, and having on the breastplate of righteousness; And your feet shod with the preparation of the gospel of peace; Above all, taking the shield of faith, wherewith ye shall be able to quench all the fiery darts of the wicked. And take the helmet of salvation, and the sword of the Spirit, which is the word of God:

'Is There Not a Cause?'

Of course, in speaking of warriors, I would be remiss if I did not mention David and his band of mighty men (2 Sam. 23:8–39). If you're thinking about a warrior in the Bible, you can't help but think about David. David was tending his father Jesse's sheep while all his older brothers were put forward by their father as potential kings of Israel. God told Samuel the prophet to pass over every one of those brothers. When Samuel asked Jesse if there were any others, he told him there was one more, the youngest, who was taking care of the sheep. Samuel sent for him and when he arrived, he anointed him king over Israel (1 Sam. 16:13). God told Samuel He chose David because he was "*a man after mine own heart*" (1 Sam. 13:14 and Acts 13:22).

In the story where he faced Goliath, his father sent him to take bread to his brothers who were in the army. When he got there, he saw that the army of Israel was cowering before a pagan giant (1 Sam. 17:17–26). This Philistine warrior, Goliath, had issued a challenge to the Israelites that threatened their nation. When David encountered this shameful situation, he said, "*Who is this uncircumcised Philistine, that he should defy the armies of the living God?*" (1 Sam. 17:26).

David's brothers began to ridicule him when he said this, which is typical of people who are too timid to stand and fight but want to criticize those who do take a stand. But David responded, "Is there *not a cause?*" (1 Sam. 17:29).

These words ought to be ringing in our ears today! Every Christian man in America should be asking himself, "Is there not a cause?" Every one of us, when we see what is happening to our nation, should ask, "How can I possibly stand back and do nothing? How can I see what's happening on television day after day and night after night and never take action?"

You see, David understood—even as a young man—that what was happening to Israel had to be opposed. Everyone else was cowering in fear, but he knew this was a time to fight. He put his trust in God, stepped into the fray, slew the giant, and set his nation free. (1 Sam. 17:48–51)

How Bad Does It Need to Get?

During the COVID pandemic, I remember when the governor of Colorado (where I live) issued an order that only essential gatherings were allowed and declared that church services were not essential.[14] When I read those words, I literally got mad inside. I thought, *How dare he? Who does he think he is? What right does he think he has to declare the sacred assembly of God's people for worship to be "nonessential." This nation was built on God, built on His Word. He obviously doesn't know anything about this country.*

I believe my reaction was one of true, righteous anger. And I believe we all need to start asking ourselves, "Who are these ungodly people trying to destroy our beloved nation? How dare they try to silence the church of Jesus Christ!" Something needs to rise up in the men of our generation to realize that every home, every school, every business, every government office is a battleground. These battles are raging not on a physical battlefield like the ones on which David fought, with an enemy we can clearly see. No, these are spiritual battles. They are battles for Truth, freedom, and the souls of human beings. Rest assured, our failure to engage will only ensure we will lose.

If you think this war is not already in your house, that you're immune or insulated from the "woke" onslaught, you are mistaken. Just take a look at your phone or your kids' phones. We are constantly bombarded with ideas and messaging through media that contain lies that will destroy you and your family. And we don't have to look far to see the fruit of these lies. Satan is marching drag queens down the streets.

Gay men—naked—are chanting, "We are coming for your children." The state of California passed a law saying that parents must give their kids mutilating, permanent, life-altering transgender surgery if their kids want it. If parents stand in the way, the state will come and take the children.[15]

Women are being forced to view men in female locker rooms.[16] Teachers now are hiding abortions and transgender therapy from parents.[17] Criminals today are allowed to go free while those who defend themselves, exercising their God-given right of self-defense, are prosecuted. Teachers and many others in America today openly embrace Marxism. The Colorado Education Association recently passed a resolution condemning capitalism as a source of evil in this nation.[18] How much worse does it need to get for men to realize that there is a cause worth fighting for?

Courage for the Battle

Where can you find courage for the battle? The answer is simple. You find courage when you have a heart of love. Jesus said,

> *Greater love hath no man than this, that a man lay down his life for his friends.*
>
> John 15:13

So, when we're talking about men being called to fight, we're not talking about fighting out of hatred for people, for revenge, or to rob and oppress others. God forbid!

Going back to 1 Corinthians 16:13 where it says to act like men, the next verse says, "*let all your things be done with charity*" (1 Cor. 16:14). The calling to fight is an integral part of what it means to be a man, and the fight men of God wage is a fight motivated by love. During the Revolutionary War, the American soldiers—made up of farmers, merchants, and ministers[19]—persevered through incredible hardship. They never stopped fighting even though they were losing far more battles than they won. They were able to keep going against all odds because they had two things: the heart of a warrior and the love of God.

Consider Valley Forge. After more than a year of fighting the British, the soldiers of General George Washington encamped for the winter of 1777 at Valley Forge, Pennsylvania. Their forces, ammunition, clothing, and supplies were depleted. As I stated before, they had lost more battles than they won. They suffered from a lack of food, inadequate shelter, and devastating diseases. At the time, the entire northern hemisphere was going through a phase of extremely cold weather that has since been dubbed "the Little Ice Age." The freedom fighters were constantly surrounded by deep snow and bitter cold. Their hardships were possibly worse than any army in the world has ever endured. But praise God, they did endure. They were able to endure because of the warrior in them. And the warrior in them was compelled by the love of God working in them for their families, their neighbors, and their nation. This was their cause! They would not stop until they had secured forever freedom from tyranny and American independence from Britain.

Americans are basically a peaceful people. We don't crave war. But in history, you can find no record of greater bravery, resilience, and tenacity than the American Armed Forces. The feats of American soldiers in battles like Guadalcanal, the Battle of the Bulge, Okinawa, Normandy, and Leyte Gulf are unmatched. America's men, especially Christian men, need to reawaken that warrior spirit. We need courageous men who will answer the call and rise up to fight! We need it no less now than in the physical wars of the past, for our families and the souls of every person in this country. Even though bullets are not flying in this country (praise God!), we are most definitely in a war. It's a war of values, principles, and ideals. It's a war of national identity and a war of Truth versus lies. In this hour, the calling to manhood is a calling to fight in this war of values, principles, and ideals. It is a calling to engage socially, politically, educationally—literally, everywhere—lest we be overcome by the enemy.

I was reading recently about General Stonewall Jackson in the Civil War. He is considered by many to be the greatest general in American history. In a letter he wrote explaining his philosophy of battle, Gen. Jackson basically said, "*What you do is find the weakest point in the enemy's lines and pursue that point. Once you breach the line, you do not relent until you have routed the enemy, until they are in utter defeat and utter retreat.*" That is God's call to Christian men everywhere today: Do not relent! Do not stop and do not compromise!

I believe God would have us be so effective in our war of Truth versus lies that we run the Enemy right off the battlefield! Let's destroy Marxism in America. Let's be so effective at standing for Truth that we completely eliminate the LGBT ideology in America. Let's destroy every racist, pagan agenda. Let's push them clean off the field of battle! We will do this, not with physical force, but by speaking, writing, and living the Truth in every area of society at every opportunity.

We need a mindset that settles for nothing less than total victory. I pray to God that not a single bullet or carnal weapon is ever deployed in this culture war, but instead, that the men of God in this land would be so skillful, relentless, and tireless in wielding the Sword of the Spirit, that the lies of the devil are exposed and rejected all over the land, from sea to shining sea!

In early August 1990, an international coalition of troops, led by the United States, launched a massive military response against the forces of Iraq's Saddam Hussein, who had invaded and occupied its neighboring nation of Kuwait. Ultimately, the coalition forces completely routed the Iraqi army from Kuwait in an impressive display of military prowess.[20] The United States suffered a relatively small number of casualties. Even though it was known that Saddam Hussein was a brutal dictator who murdered thousands of his own people, U.S. President George H.W. Bush chose to stop the military advance at the Iraq border. He refused to topple Hussein in Iraq.

Just a few years later, however, his son, President George W. Bush, had to invade Iraq because he was persuaded that Hussein possessed "weapons of mass destruction" and gave aid to the terrorists who attacked America on September 11, 2001. This became known as the Iraq War and cost over 4,000 American lives.[21] It would have been much easier and less costly to have pressed the attack in the first Gulf War when we were fully mobilized and had the momentum.

In this culture war we are facing today, we need to press the attack all the way through to completion. We cannot accept or accommodate anything other than total victory. Even if we make good progress, if we stop short of fully discipling our nation, the disease of thought and mind that is plaguing us will rise up again. With truth, love, courage, and hard work, we've got to pluck up the lying philosophies, roots and all, and reestablish America on the principles on which it was founded. Men, let us all rise up and declare with conviction, "No matter the cost, I will not stand by and watch the destruction of my nation. I am going to enter the battle and fight for the glory of God and love of my country and my family!"

Chapter Four
The Call to Work!

The third calling to manhood that God has given every single man is the call to work. Simply put, men are designed by God to work and to work hard.

There are physiological differences between men and women to reflect distinctions in purpose. They are too many for me to cover, but it is worth pointing out that men do not bear children, only women can do that. Women have several physical traits that make them better at certain things than men, including the ability to read emotions, discern color variations, engage in intuitive reasoning, and produce greater volumes of verbal communication. However, men have more muscle mass, larger bones, and testosterone. They generally discern objects in motion with greater accuracy and can exclude unwanted sounds from conscious attention more easily. These differences, and many others, are not accidental. They reflect distinction of purpose.

One of the core purposes of men is to work. It is very telling that when God pronounced the curses on Adam and Eve after their sin, Eve was cursed with pain in childbirth and Adam was cursed with travail as he worked the ground (Genesis 3). I believe the Lord chose these because they represent core callings for each sex.

We should also consider these Bible verses:

Six days thou shalt work, but on the seventh day thou shalt rest: in earing time and in harvest thou shalt rest.

Exodus 34:21

The hand of the diligent shall bear rule: but the slothful shall be under tribute.

Proverbs 12:24

Men have a God-infused design to seek to accomplish things. We naturally like to build and tear down, to design, fix, invent, and improve. We can love and value people intensely but grow impatient with too much talking and face time. When two women want to spend time together, often they will make some tea and sit together on a couch talking for a couple of hours. When two men want to spend time together, they go play golf, hunt, fish, or do a project together. When men see a problem, their first reaction is to try to fix it, not to talk about how the problem makes people feel. Women bond best when face to face. Men bond with others best when they are side by side.

One of the reasons men in this generation are floundering is because our feminized culture has diminished their roles as providers for their families. For fifty years, men in the West have been told that women can do everything they can do. We have adopted government welfare programs that have made man's role as provider in the home unnecessary.

Man the Post

You might be frustrated when you look around today because it seems like the wrong people are in office. Or maybe you get angry because we have judges who won't follow the Constitution. Or perhaps you are discouraged because there's so much corruption going on in America today. But I want to say to you, if you are frustrated, angry, and discouraged, why don't you get up and do something about it? The Bible says that the hand of the diligent will bear rule (Prov. 12:24). If you want your opinions and ideas to rule, then get to work on it!

I would like to suggest that one of the main reasons we are seeing a deterioration of our culture today is because the

Church of Jesus Christ, especially its men, has abandoned its posts.

Jesus said, "*The harvest truly* is *great, but the labourers are few: pray ye therefore the Lord of the harvest, that he would send forth labourers into his harvest*" (Luke 10:2).

Figuratively speaking, instead of working God's field—the earth—most men in the Church have left the field to go into town and hang out at the local pub. The field has been wide open for decades and the wicked are now plundering God's harvest. And I promise you, unlike many Christian men, the wicked have been working night and day for a long time to get their harvest.

I read an article the other day about a study that was done on political activity among religious groups. The study concluded that *atheists* in America are the hardest-working political group. They engage in twice as many activities monthly as some demographics of evangelical Christians.[22] They also give twice as much money to political candidates. It's no wonder that people like George Soros and Jeff Bezos are running circles around the church. But the body of Christ can do better if we reclaim our posts. We can put these people to shame.

Historically, Americans have had the greatest work ethic in the Western world. It came out of love and a sense of individual responsibility. Because of our sense of freedom under God, we also understood individual responsibility. Americans have known, "It's up to me to make my life better. It's up to me to make my community better. It's up to me to make my nation better." Carrying these ideas in their hearts, Americans have tamed a vast wilderness and built the most prosperous and innovative nation in the history of the world. There is no comparison between the United States of America and any other country or empire that has been before.

American history is filled with pioneers and explorers, from expeditioners like Lewis and Clark to astronauts like Neil Armstrong and Gus Grissom. American optimism, rooted in our faith in God, fueled an individual work ethic that has built the greatest economy in the world. Although we have only four percent of the world's population, our Gross Domestic Product ($25 trillion) is the world's highest and represents twenty-four percent of the entire economic output of the planet.

America has led the world in inventions and technology. Americans invented the lightbulb, the telephone, the telegraph, the airplane, the smartphone, the assembly line, the personal computer, the semiconductor, lasers, copy machines, MRIs, chemotherapy, and the global positioning system (GPS), just to name a few. America once had a public education system that was a model for the world. We lead the world in patents and have three times more Nobel Prize winners than the next highest country.

Despite this incredible legacy, America seems to be losing its preeminence. China already has the largest military in the world and will soon have the largest economy, if America does not get its house in order. Our national debt is now $35 trillion, a figure so large that it can hardly be conceived. As each day passes, our debt grows and consumes a larger portion of our national budget.

I mention these things because they can all be traced back to men losing their calling to lead, fight, and work. Surveys demonstrate the declining work ethic in America's younger generation. The actions of our politicians are a reflection of the citizens who put them there. The politicians have failed to do what is responsible and right (cut spending, pay off debt, and balance the budget for example) because the people care more about government handouts and spending in their districts than they do about character and fiscal responsibility. The men of our country need to take their place, real men, that is, to lead based on principle and character, to fight for what is good and right in the public square, and to build wealth through work and patience like the Bible says (Prov. 10:4). If the men of our country fulfilled their calling to true manhood, we would put a stop to these things and get things back on track. If we're going to take this nation back, men must rediscover their God-given calling to work.

Get the Salt Out of the Shaker

Following Jesus is not a nine-to-five, Monday through Friday job. The words "weekend" and "job" are of modern origin. You can't find them in the Bible. The truth is that if America is going to be taken back, it's going to take a lot of hard work, for which you might not even be paid or thanked. God is calling men to go beyond the nine to five and do things like volunteer for political campaigns, knock on doors, make phone calls, attend meetings, go to school board meetings, go to town hall meetings, lead youth groups, and start Constitution clubs in church.

The salt has to get out of the saltshaker. Remember, Jesus said, "*Ye are the salt of the earth: but if the salt have lost his savour, wherewith shall it be salted? It is thenceforth good for nothing, but to be cast out, and to be trodden under foot of men*" (Matt. 5:13). Men, you were made for more than you might realize. You have more responsibility than just your job and family. Christian men, you are the solution to the problems of the world, but you can't make a difference without putting in the work.

Repairing the Walls

I'm continually reminded of the story of Nehemiah, a man who was moved to action by news about the condition of his country (Neh. 2:1–3). He was a Jew in exile, serving the King of Persia. When he heard people come to the royal court and report on how the holy city of Jerusalem lay in ruins, it broke his heart (Neh. 1:2–4). He sought permission from the king to go to Jerusalem and rebuild its wall. By God's hand, he was given that permission (Neh. 2:5–8). However, when he got there, he knew the job wasn't going to be easy. There was great opposition and many enemies occupied the land (Neh. 2:9–20). Nevertheless, Nehemiah instilled in his people a willingness to fight and to work (Neh. 4:6). And because of his leadership, every man took his place on the wall, with a sword on his hip and a trowel in his hand (Neh. 4:17–18). The Bible says that these men refused to even go home at night (Neh. 4:21–23). They slept inside the rubble of the walls to keep the work safe and secure from those who hated the Jews and wanted to keep Jerusalem in ruins. Sleep in the rubble. Now, that is commitment to work!

Realizing the opposition these men were facing, consider what Nehemiah did:

> *Therefore set I in the lower places behind the wall, and on the higher places, I even set the people after their families with their swords, their spears, and their bows. And I looked, and rose up, and said unto the nobles, and to the rulers, and to the rest of the people, Be not ye afraid of them: remember the Lord, which is great and terrible, and fight for your brethren, your sons, and your daughters, your wives, and your houses.*
>
> Nehemiah 4:13–14

This is such an inspirational example of what I've been sharing with you in this booklet: Just like the men of Israel under Nehemiah, you too are called to lead, to fight, and to work! If Nehemiah lived in our generation today, he would say, "Don't worry about what the news media says. Don't be afraid of liberals. Pay no attention to the criticism of the ungodly, or those who hate Jesus Christ and the Word of God. But remember who you are as sons of God! Stand up and fight for your families, your communities, and your nation!"

God is calling us to be men no less now than when he called Nehemiah all those years ago. And he is calling every one of us to lead, to fight, and to work "*for your brethren, your sons, and your daughters, your wives, and your houses*" (Neh. 4:14). We can no longer sit by and expect the job to be done by others. It is up to us!

Conclusion

The Founding Fathers faced a crisis and they courageously rose to meet it. They pledged themselves to achieve victory or die trying. Today in America, we are once again facing a crisis. This crisis is threatening the very existence of the country we call home. In a way, I want every Christian man in America to take this threat personally. Most Christian men I know would put themselves in harm's way to protect their loved ones and their homes. Our problem is, although we are seeing the "woke" and corrupt things going on in our culture, while we may not like it and may be annoyed by it, we don't really see it as a *personal* threat to the people and things we hold dear. But the truth is, the things going on in our country today *are a direct threat to every family in the country*. There is an unholy alliance of Marxists, racists, LGBT radicals, and Islamic jihadi forces that are working together to destroy America. They do not believe in the principles of the Declaration of Independence or the Constitution. They have no respect for evangelical Christianity or the authority of the Bible. They want to remove guns, strip parents of authority, spread homosexuality and transgenderism to children, impose communism, revise our history books, open our borders, subject us to global governing powers, control all aspects of medical care, abort our unborn children, euthanize the elderly, and silence all who disagree with their agenda, especially Christians. The spirit of antichrist is behind them and he will not stop until he has literally exterminated the gospel from the planet.

As bad as the danger is, I have great hope. I believe we're beginning to see the tide shift. There is a lot of good happening in America, too, and we are gaining momentum.

On a recent Truth & Liberty show, we started talking about some of the amazing things that are happening in America right now. For example, a slate of decisions came out of the United States Supreme Court in recent years that have been absolutely awesome. We are making great strides in re-establishing the Constitution as it was intended: freedom of speech, freedom of religion, and separation of powers, to name a few. I told the guest who was with me on the live show, "It feels like God is righting the ship!" And He is. But He has also given us a window to shore up the things He is doing and see the job finished.

We have the power and ability, with God's help, to turn this nation around. It's already started, but we need to be like Stonewall Jackson; we need to say, "There's a breach in the line! We will not quit, we will not give up, and we are going to pursue this thing to total victory!" That is one of the main purposes for this booklet. It's a word for today!

So, I want to ask you today, men, will you lead? Will you stand up and enter the fight? Will you stand up and get to work? Will you act like a man in your generation, like the American Forefathers did in theirs?

You might ask, "Where can I start?" There are a variety of ways you can get involved. But choose to get involved. Choose to stand up, speak up, and show up. If you make that choice, you can start looking around for opportunities to make a difference for Truth. I guarantee you won't have to look far.

Maybe you should be vocal about biblical values on social media more often. Maybe you should volunteer to coach your kid's soccer team. Maybe, you should join a civic organization where you can stand for Truth. Maybe you need to get educated about American history and God's view of government. Maybe you should get involved in your local Republican party, or volunteer for a candidate to knock on doors and make phone calls. Maybe you can circulate petitions to restrict abortion or ban boys from playing in girls' sports. Maybe you should start a Community Impact team or a Biblical Citizenship course in your local church. Maybe you should run for local office, like school board or town council.

No matter what you do, the important thing is to get started doing something. A ship that's not moving cannot be steered. If you get moving, God will be faithful to direct you into the field of labor where He wants you. When He does, it will be fun, exciting, and rewarding!

You can go to the Truth & Liberty website at **TruthandLiberty.net** and explore our resources page. We have hundreds of links to inform you about things you can do that would be transformative to your community. You can also sign up to be a volunteer for Truth & Liberty. We have numerous ways to get involved, including distributing voter guides in Colorado. These voter guides will educate the public about school board candidates. We have many other ways for you to make a difference across the nation. I ask you to prayerfully consider getting involved with what we're doing here. You don't have to start from scratch; you can join the movement that's already started. I promise you'll be blessed to make a real impact in this generation.

We as men have got to do what God has made, designed, and destined us to do. Let it not be said of this generation that we didn't answer the call. But let us be like the sons of Issachar "[Who] were *valiant men of might in their generations*" (1 Chron. 7:2, brackets mine).

Let me pray for you.

"We love You, Lord. We praise You, Jesus. You are the perfect Man. You are the Man of men. You're the Son of God. And we as men want to be like You. We set our hearts and minds on You. And just like You stepped into the fray—You didn't run or hide from the opposition—and gave Your life for us on the cross, may we also rise up to meet the threats to our faith, our families, and our freedom. Right now, Lord, our country is under attack like we've never seen before. But we give ourselves to You for this cause. I ask and pray that You would reveal to the man reading this booklet how he's called to lead, to fight, and to work, in Jesus' name. Amen."

Now pray this out loud:

"Dear God, I promise today before You and my family that I will lead my family, I will fight for my family, and I will work for my family in the place that You show me. No matter the cost, no matter the price. Lord, I will be faithful, in Jesus' name. Amen."

Endnotes

1. *National Archives*, "Signers of the Declaration of Independence," accessed on March 22, 2024, https://www.archives.gov/founding-docs/signers-factsheet.

2. Walter Isaacson, "Benjamin Franklin Joins the Revolution," Smithsonian Magazine, July 31, 2003, https://www.smithsonianmag.com/history/benjamin-franklin-joins-the-revolution-87199988/.

3. *U.S. History Online Textbook*, "Loyalists, Fence-sitters, and Patriots," ushistory.org, accessed March 22, 2024, www.ushistory.org/us/11b.asp.

4. *Strong's Definitions*, s.v. "ἀνδρίζομαι" ("andrízomai"), accessed May 29, 2024, https://www.blueletterbible.org/lexicon/g407/kjv/tr/0-1/

5. Weizmann Institute of Science, "Researchers identify 6,500 genes that are expressed differently in men and women," *Science Daily*, May 4, 2017, https://www.sciencedaily.com/releases/2017/05/170504104342.htm; Steven Wedgeworth, "The Science of Male and Female," *Desiring God*, September 11, 2020, https://www.sciencedaily.com/releases/2017/05/170504104342.htm.

6. *60 Minutes*, "Hillary Clinton's First 60 Minutes Interview," *YouTube*, 1992, accessed March 22, 2024, https://www.youtube.com/watch?v=-UqKNgrwK8E.

7. Fox News, "Twitter laughs, groans as Jill Biden gives biological male Woman of Courage award: 'Up your game ladies'," March 8, 2023, https://www.foxnews.com/media/twitter-laughs-groans-jill-biden-gives-biological-male-women-courage-award-game-ladies.

8. NCAA, "Transgender Student-Athlete Participation Policy," April 17, 2023, https://www.ncaa.org/sports/2022/1/27/transgender-participation-policy.aspx; David Gortler, "Allowing Biological Males in Women's Sports is Scientifically Unsound," Ethics & Public Policy Center, October 6, 2022, https://eppc.org/publication/allowing-biological-males-in-womens-sports-is-scientifically-unsound/.

9. Matthew Impelli, "Audrey Hale's Manifesto Details Monthslong Plan to Commit Shooting," Newsweek, April 3, 2023, https://www.newsweek.com/audrey-hales-manifesto-details-monthslong-plan-commit-shooting-1792317.

10. The White House, "A Proclamation on Transgender Day of Visibility," March 30, 2023, https://www.whitehouse.gov/briefing-room/presidential-actions/2023/03/30/a-proclamation-on-transgender-day-of-visibility/.

11. George Washington's Mount Vernon, "Biography of George Washington," accessed March 22, 2024, https://www.mountvernon.org/george-washington/biography/, and "Churchwarden and Vestryman," accessed March 22,

2024, https://www.mountvernon.org/george-washington/religion/churchwarden-and-vestryman/.

12. Jake Brewer, "ISSUE BRIEF: Fatherlessness and its effects on American Society," America First Policy Institute, May 15, 2023, https://americafirstpolicy.com/issues/issue-brief-fatherlessness-and-its-effects-on-american-society.

13. John Stevey, "The Special Forces Prayer," AUSA, February 28, 2017, https://www.ausa.org/special-forces-prayer, and SFA Chapter 46 "Col Nick Rowe Memorial Chapter," "Special Forces Creed, Prayer, and Overview," accessed May 29, 2024, https://sfachapter46.com/sf-creed-prayer-overview#:~:text=fight%20against%20terrorism.-,Special%20Forces%20Prayer,and%20to%20free%20the%20enslaved.

14. Colorado Governor Jared Polis, "2020 Executive Orders," accessed March 22, 2024, https://www.colorado.gov/governor/2020-executive-orders; Robert Davis, "Revised public health order loosens restrictions on Colorado churches, educational institutions, and bars," *Kiowa County Press*, December 10, 2020, https://kiowacountypress.net/content/revised-public-health-order-loosens-restrictions-colorado-churches-educational-institutions.

15. Anthony Cash, "California Bill Would Classify Not Affirming Child's Transgenderism As 'Child Abuse,'" *Daily Wire*, June 9, 2023, https://www.dailywire.com/news/california-bill-would-classify-not-affirming-childs-transgenderism-as-child-abuse

16. Alec Schemmel, "Trans Student Exposed Girls to Male Genitalia in School Locker Room, Legal Group Claims," April 21, 2023, WPDE-TV, https://wpde.com/news/nation-world/after-trans-woman-exposed-genitalia-to-freshman-girls-in-locker-room-shower-school-district-faces-legal-scrutiny

17. Jackie Salo, "Washington Teacher Gives Out Flyers Advising Kids on Abortions Without Parental Consent: Report," *New York Post*, June 29, 2021, https://nypost.com/2021/06/29/teacher-gives-out-flyers-advising-kids-on-abortions-without-consent/ and Tony Kinnett, "'What Else Are They Willing to Lie About?': Indiana School Compels Staff to Hide 'Gender Support Plans' From Parents," Daily Signal, December 5, 2022, https://www.dailysignal.com/2022/12/05/indiana-school-compels-counselors-teachers-to-hide-gender-support-plans-from-parents/

18. John Ranson, "State teachers' union admits Marxist platform points from assembly, *The Lion*, Herzog Foundation, May 3, 2023, https://readlion.com/state-teachers-union-admits-marxist-platform-points-from-assembly/.

19. American Battlefield Trust, "The Fighting Man of the Continental Army," November 28, 2023, https://www.battlefields.org/learn/articles/fighting-man-continental-army.

20. Naval History and Heritage Command, "Desert Shield/Desert Storm," accessed May 29, 2024. https://www.history.navy.mil/browse-by-topic/wars-conflicts-and-operations/middle-east/shield-storm.html.

21. Nicholas Anastacio and Mark Murray, "The Iraq War - by the Numbers," NBCNews.com, March 20, 2023. https://www.nbcnews.com/meet-the-press/meetthepressblog/iraq-war-numbers-rcna75762.

22. Ryan Burge, "Religious Right? Those true believers are nowhere near as politically active as atheists," *Get Religion*, May 31, 2024, https://www.getreligion.org/getreligion/2023/5/29/religious-right-those-true-believers-are-nowhere-near-as-politically-active-as-atheists.

About the Author

Richard Harris serves as the Executive Director of the Truth & Liberty Coalition, based in Woodland Park, Colorado. Truth & Liberty, founded by world-renowned bible teacher Andrew Wommack, has become an influential voice in our nation, calling the Body of Christ to stand for truth in the seven mountains of cultural influence.

Richard co-hosts the Truth & Liberty Live Cast every week and spearheads Truth & Liberty's work to educate, unify, and mobilize Christians through media, grassroots activism, inspirational conferences, and strategic collaboration.

Richard is also the founder of Richard Harris Ministries, a bible-teaching ministry dedicated to making disciples of Jesus Christ by teaching the Gospel of Grace and the Word of God.

Richard is a licensed attorney who, after graduating magna cum laude from Cornell University Law School, actively practiced law for twenty-seven years. Richard has represented clients at all levels of state and federal courts, including the United States Supreme Court. He recently served as the General Counsel for Andrew Wommack Ministries, Inc. He has a passion for seeing restoration of America's constitutional republic under God. Using in large part the research and writings of David Barton and WallBuilders, Richard was instrumental in building the curriculum and plan of study for the Practical Government School at Charis Bible College, a program he also administered for three years.

He and his wife Donna have three amazing sons.

 TRUTH & LIBERTY

Truth & Liberty is a non-profit based in Woodland Park, Colorado. Established by Andrew Wommack and other Christian leaders, we seek to educate, unify and mobilize believers in Jesus to affect the reformation of nations through the seven mountains of cultural influence.

Our heart is to mobilize the church to engage with biblical truth. Our goal is to educate our audience and connect them with resources and organizations across the nation to help them impact their own spheres of influence.

Truth & Liberty stands for preserving America's constitutional republic of government from the consent of the governed through democratically elected representatives for the purpose of guaranteeing to each citizen their Creator-given rights.

For more information about Truth & Liberty visit **Truthandliberty.net**

Contact Information

Truth and Liberty
1 Innovation Way
Woodland Park, CO 80863
info@truthandliberty.net
TruthandLiberty.net

Andrew Wommack Ministries, Inc.
PO Box 3333
Colorado Springs, CO 80934-3333
info@awmi.net
awmi.net
Helpline: 719-635-1111 (available 24/7)

Charis Bible College
info@charisbiblecollege.org
844-360-9577
CharisBibleCollege.org
For a complete list of all of our offices,
visit **awmi.net/contact-us**.

Connect with us on social media.